THE CUTEST PUPPIES EVER!

Authors: Catherine Veitch & Anna Claybourne
Designers: Mike Henson & James Handlon
Editor: Harriet Stone

This library edition published by Quarto Library,
an imprint of The Quarto Group.
26391 Crown Valley Parkway, Suite 220
Mission Viejo, CA 92691, USA
T: +1 949 380 7510
F: +1 949 380 7575
www.QuartoKnows.com

Distributed in the United States and Canada by
Lerner Publisher Services
241 First Avenue North
Minneapolis, MN 55401 U.S.A.
www.lernerbooks.com

A CIP record for this book is available from the
Library of Congress.

ISBN 978-0-7112-7230-9

Manufactured in Guangdong,
China TT082021

9 8 7 6 5 4 3 2 1

Puppy Stats contain
information on color,
size, and cuteness
rating, plus a quick fact
about each breed.

PUPPY STATS

Color: White, black,
silver
Size: Tiny

A little dog with
a big voice!

CONTENTS

**Which is the cutest of them all?
Read on and find out!**

LABRADOR RETRIEVER

The Labrador Retriever is a friendly, playful breed—and as a bouncy, cuddly puppy, she's even more fun!

Labrador puppies just love rolling around, play-fighting, and chasing things. They have warm, open faces and big, adoring eyes.

Labradors were bred to retrieve (fetch) things from water, so they like getting wet, too.

PUPPY STATS

Color: All colors
Size: Large

♥ ♥ ♥ ♥ ♥

★ These dogs were used to hunt wild boar and deer.

BORZOI

Sweet, sensible, and laid-back—that's a Borzoi puppy. Until she sees something to chase, that is, and then she zooms off at incredible speed!

In Russia, where this breed comes from, the name "Borzoi" means "fast."

Borzoi pups are also affectionate, and love to cuddle in your lap—even though they're a bit too big!

PUPPY STATS

Color: Many colors
Size: Huge

A Borzoi's nose takes three years to grow into the long nose of an adult.

MINIATURE SCHNAUZER

What could be more adorable than a tiny puppy with a big beard and mustache!?

Miniature Schnauzers are friendly, feisty puppies with a serious fluffiness factor. They're always over the moon to see you, and will make you laugh by chasing things and trying to get your attention.

PUPPY STATS

Color: White, black, silver
Size: Tiny

A little dog with a big voice!

GREYHOUND

Greyhounds are
FAST runners.
Even the puppies
have long legs,
sleek bodies,
and love chasing
anything they can.

Once they've had a good run, Greyhound pups are calm, sweet, and gentle.

A Greyhound's short hair means it can get chilly. So if it's cold, get your Greyhound pup a cozy coat!

PUPPY STATS

Color: Many colors
Size: Big

Most Greyhounds like to lie down rather than sit because of how their bodies are made.

PUG

It's no surprise that this wrinkly-faced pup's favorite place is right by your side, because pugs were bred in China as lapdogs for royalty.

Pugs love snoozing and snoring indoors. But they like to go out for short walks, too, when it's not too hot or too cold.

PUPPY STATS

Color: Fawn, black, silver
Size: Tiny

A group of pugs is called a "grumble!"

POODLE

People often think of Poodles as fluffy, pretty, and cute, with their soft curly coats and sweet eyes. And they certainly are!

But a Poodle pup is no slouch. These puppies are great at running, jumping, and leaping around obstacle courses.

They're also super-smart, and love to interact, play, and learn new tricks.

PUPPY STATS

Color: Many colors
Size: From tiny to LARGE

A Poodle's fur never stops growing, so it needs trips to the groomer often!

CHIHUAHUA

This Chihuahua may be pocket-sized but she has a big personality and you will know when there's a Chihuahua around!

Chihuahuas love to burrow and will snuggle under anything including blankets, pillows, and dirty clothes. They also feel the cold so put a sweater on your pup in cold weather.

PUPPY STATS

Color: Many colors
Size: Tiny

Chihuahuas are named after the place in Mexico where they came from.

AMERICAN STAFFORDSHIRE TERRIER

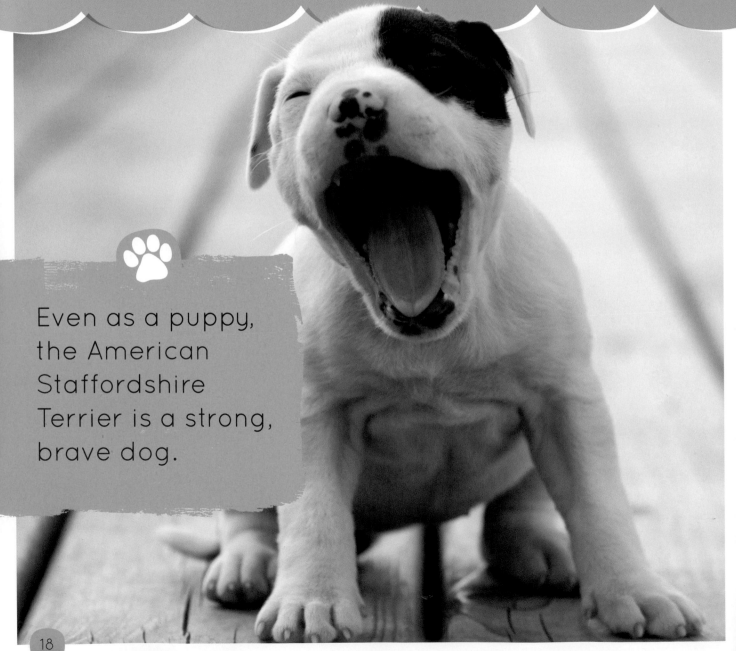

Even as a puppy, the American Staffordshire Terrier is a strong, brave dog.

People are sometimes scared of these puppies because of their big jaws, but they are one of the most easygoing, good-natured doggies you could meet.

They'll bounce everywhere, jump up to greet you, and give you a big slobbery kiss!

PUPPY STATS

Color: White, tan, black
Size: Medium

♡ ♥ ♥ ♡

⭐ Give your staffie pup the toughest chew toys to keep her strong jaws busy!

CORGI

With his short, stubby legs, eager face, and fluffy fur, a Corgi pup is like a real live plush doggy toy!

Corgis aren't just cute though—they are reliable, brave dogs who like to guard their family home.

They love children, but watch out: a Corgi pup can sometimes be naughty and give you a nip!

PUPPY STATS

Color: Light brown, red, black, white
Size: Medium

Corgis are a favorite with the British queen!

IRISH WOLFHOUND

An Irish Wolfhound puppy is a big, lovable buffoon with a funny face and incredibly cute, pleading eyes.

These sweet, gentle dogs have very long legs, and as puppies, they're often adorably clumsy and goofy. They also need lots of strokes and hugs.

They don't make good guard dogs though—they're too soft!

PUPPY STATS

Color: Many colors
Size: Huge

🤍 🤍 🤍

⭐ They can grow to seven feet tall standing on their back legs!

PAPILLON

This breed is named the "Papillon," meaning butterfly, thanks to its big, beautiful, butterfly-shaped ears.

Papillon puppies are bright and friendly. They are fast learners, and love playing games with their owners.

They're so small, sweet, and well-behaved, this is the kind of pup you might see a movie star carrying in her handbag!

PUPPY STATS

Color: Black, brown, white
Size: Tiny

Watch your puppy's silky hair grow as it gets older, especially on its ears.

GERMAN SHEPHERD

So sweet and fluffy, this gorgeous puppy will grow into a confident, brave, and devoted dog.

The German Shepherd is one of the most popular pet dogs of all. These pups love to run, jump, fetch, and play.

They're smart and make great police dogs, guard dogs, guide dogs, and rescue dogs.

PUPPY STATS

Color: Black, light brown, white
Size: Large

★ Those goofy, floppy ears will stand upright when they're grown up.

VIZSLA

You can see in this puppy's big, wise eyes just how smart and thoughtful he is.

A Vizsla pup is quick to learn, with a great sense of smell—they often become working sniffer dogs. What they want most is to be around people, and to be stroked, petted, and loved. Awww!

PUPPY STATS

Color: Shades of gold
Size: Big

♥ ♥ ♥ ♥

⭐ Like to exercise their minds and bodies.

DACHSHUND

This cutie is also known as a doxie or a sausage dog.

Dachshunds LOVE to eat, so be careful you don't overfeed your little pup, however cute he looks!

These are loyal dogs and will bond closely to one person. They like to have all of your attention and may bark at unexpected visitors.

PUPPY STATS

Color: Many colors
Size: From miniature to small

Dachshunds live for a long time. One lived for a record-breaking 21 years!

PICTURE ACKNOWLEDGMENTS

BC = back cover, FC = front cover, b = below, c = center,
l = left, r = right

Alamy: 12 Ariane Lohmar/imageBROKER; 15 (main) Ivaylo Sarayski; 21 (main) MIXA/SOURCENEXT; 23br WILDLIFE GmbH; 23 (main) Juniors Bildarchiv / F421/ Juniors Bildarchiv GmbH. **Dreamstime:** 17bc Anke Van Wyk; 25 (main) Sergey Lavrentev; 30 Xalanx. **FLPA:** 4 ImageBROKER; 31bc Jeanette Hutfluss/Tierfotoagentur/ FLPA; 31 (main) Imagebroker, Friedhelm Adam/FLPA. **Getty Images:** 6 Zuzana Uhlikova; 7 (main) KUNIAKI OKADA/amanaimagesRF; 11 (main) Narelle. Sartain, alternate take photography AU; 14 bingdian; 17 (main) knape; 20 Paul Park; 29bc VJDora; 29 (main) Jessica Lynn Culver. **istockphoto:** 11bl igartist; 18 Laures. **Shutterstock:** BC Orientgold; FC Natalia Fedosova; 1 titiya chuaichat; 2-3 Lunja; 5 (main); 5 cl Mila Atkovska; 7cr Natalia Fedosova; 8 MaraZe; 9bc MaraZe; 9 (main) Stephanie Frey; 10 New Africa; 13bc alekuwka; 13 (main) spartasibe; 15bc PCHT; 16 Steve Pepple; 19bc Aneta Jungerova; 19 (main) Canon Boy; 21bl Rita Kochmarjova; 22 Zuzule; 24 BIGANDT.COM; 25bc Malivan_Iuliia; 26 Lurin; 27br Hugo Felix; 27 (main) Rita Kochmarjova; 28 Zuzule; 32 Jagodka.